PRIMARY PRAISE

60 Scripture Songs for Kids

Compiled by Ken Bible

Advisory Committee:

Joseph Linn
Lyndell Leatherman
David McDonald
Wilma Wilson
Evelyn Beals

Lillenas PUBLISHING COMPANY

KANSAS CITY, MO 64141

1

I Will Enter His Gates

LEONA VON BRETHORST

(Ps. 100:4; 118:24)

LEONA VON BRETHORST

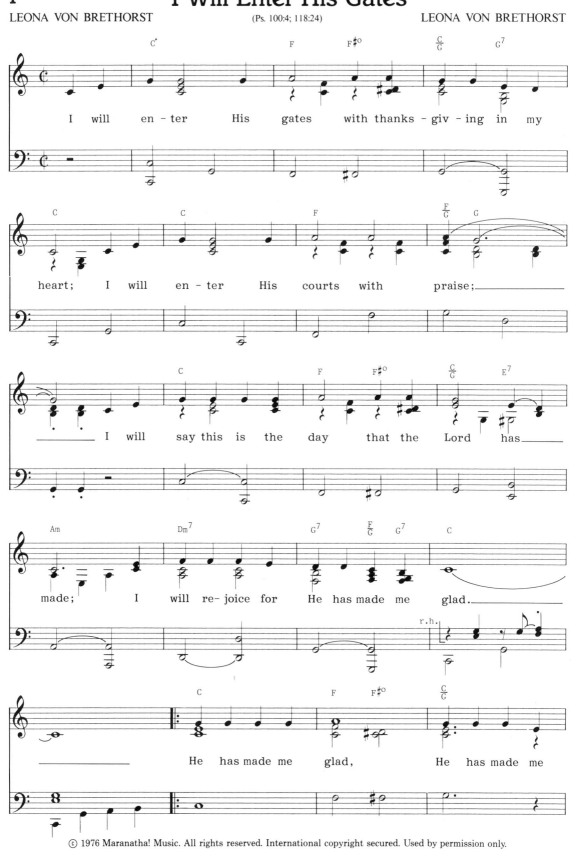

I will en-ter His gates with thanks-giv-ing in my heart; I will en-ter His courts with praise; I will say this is the day that the Lord has made; I will re-joice for He has made me glad. He has made me glad, He has made me

King of Kings

2

SOPHIE CONTY and
NAOMI BATYA

(Is.9:6; Rev.19:16)

Ancient Hebrew Folksong

glad;   I will re - joice for He has made me glad.

He   has made me   glad.

King of Kings and Lord of Lords, glo-ry, hal-le-lu-jah! Je-sus,

Prince of Peace, glo-ry, hal-le-lu-jah! Je-sus, Prince of Peace,

glo-ry, hal-le-lu-jah!   glo-ry, hal-le-lu-jah!

3

A-B-C-D-E-F-G

(John 3:16)

H.M.

HUGH MITCHELL

Fishers of Men

(Matt. 4:19; 11:28)

H.C.

HARRY CLARKE

tacet

1. I will make you fish-ers of men, fish-ers of men,
2. Hear Christ call - ing, "Come un - to Me. come un - to Me,

fish-ers of men. I will make you fish-ers of men if you
come un - to Me." Hear Christ call - ing, "Come un - to Me; I will

fol - low Me. If you fol - low
give you rest. I will give you

Me, if you fol - low Me; I will
rest; I will give you rest." Hear Christ

make you fish-ers of men if you fol - low Me.
call - ing, "Come un - to Me; I will give you rest."

5 Creature Praise

(Ps. 148:7,10; 150:6)

DAVID MATTHEWS

6

I'm Something Special

(Ps.139:13-14)

WILLIAM J. and GLORIA GAITHER

WILLIAM J. GAITHER

With a shuffle

(Boys) 1. I have a lit-tle sis-ter who's not at all like me; She can
(Girls) 2. My dad-dy mows the back yard; my moth-er makes the bed; My

write a love-ly po-em, but I can climb a tree. My
broth-er cleans the play-room; I see the dog gets fed. And

broth-er too is dif-f'rent, with freck-les on his nose; When my
each one needs the oth-er to help him thro' the day, And

ques-tions need-ed an-swers, he's the one who knows.
love must be the rea-son God planned it just that way.

7

Say to the Lord, I Love You

E.R. and D.K.

(Ps.116:1)

ERNIE RETTINO
and DEBBY KERNER

8

Stop, Go, Watch

(Matt.24: 30-31,42; 28:18-20; Acts 1:8)

*1. Stop, and let me tell you what the Lord has done for me.
*2. Go, and tell the sto-ry of the Christ of Cal-va-ry.
3. Watch, and be ye read-y for the Lord may come to-day.

Stop, and let me tell you what the Lord has done for
Go, and tell the sto-ry of the Christ of Cal-va-
Watch, and be ye read-y for the Lord may come to-

me. He for-gave my sin and He saved my soul,____ He
ry. He'll for-give their sins, He will save their souls;____ He'll
day. He will come a-gain in the clouds for me_____ and

cleansed my heart and He made me whole. Stop, and let me
cleanse their hearts, He will make them whole. Go, and tell the
take me home for e-ter-ni-ty. Watch, and be ye

tell you what the Lord has done for me.
sto-ry of the Christ of Cal-va-ry.
read-y for the Lord may come to-day.

*Verses 1 and 2 on recording.

9 Give Me Joy in My Heart

(Mark 11:9-10; Gal.5:22)

Traditional

Traditional
Arr. by Joseph Linn

1. Give me joy in my heart, keep me prais-ing._____ Give me joy in my heart, I pray. Give me joy in my heart, keep me prais-ing._____ Keep me prais-ing till the break of day.
2. Give me peace in my heart, keep me lov-ing._____ Give me peace in my heart, I pray. Give me peace in my heart, keep me lov-ing._____ Keep me lov-ing till the break of day.
3. Give me love in my heart, keep me serv-ing._____ Give me love in my heart, I pray. Give me love in my heart, keep me serv-ing._____ Keep me serv-ing till the break of day.

10 We Were Made to Love the Lord

(Gen. 1; Matt. 22:36-38)

K. H. and J. McM.

KATHIE HILL and JANET McMAHAN

*1. God made birds to fill the skies,_____ God made frogs to eat the flies,_____ God made owls_____ to just look wise,_____
2. God made fish to swim the seas,_____ God made squirrels to climb the trees,_____ God made dogs_____ to car - ry fleas,_____
*3. God made foxes to be real trick-y, God made worms to feel real stick-y, God made spi-ders to just be yick-y,

REFRAIN

But we were made to love the Lord. Yes, we were made to love the Lord,_____ love the Lord,_____ love the Lord._____

1, 2: D.S.
3: Fine

We were made to love the Lord;_____ that's what we were made for.

*Verses 1 & 3 on recording.

If You Can Sing a Song

(Ps. 149:1)

P. J. and H. J.

PETER and HANNEKE JACOBS

Option: Teacher may sing first part of phrases, with children joining in on "(then) praise the Lord." Children would do according to the teacher's words.

12 A Great Big God

(Gen. 1; Isa. 66:2)

M. P.

MARK PENDERGRASS

1. You hung all the stars and named them one by one; You rolled out the moon and lit the sun. Tip-ping up the moun-tains, pour-ing out the sea; Then You turned a-round and You made me. You're a

2. You con-trol the thun-der, cause the wind to blow, Send the driv-ing rain and si-lent snow; O-pen ev-'ry flow-er, col-or ev-'ry tree; Then You sit right down and talk to me. You're a

REFRAIN

13 This Is the Day

(Ps. 118:24)

L. G.

LES GARRETT

Option: After the song is learned, divide the children into two groups. One group sings statement, and the other group sings echoing phrase. All would sing the [bracketed] words together.

14 Faith

F.H. and S.S.P.

(Heb.11:6)

FRANK HERNANDEZ and
SHERRY SAUNDERS POWELL

Without faith it's im-pos-si-ble,___ it's im-pos-si-ble,___ it's im-pos-si-ble___ to please God. He who comes to God must be-lieve that He is, and He re-wards those who seek Him. All things are pos-si-ble,___ all things are pos-si-ble,___ all things are pos-si-ble;___ just be-lieve. God will do ev-'ry-thing that He

says He will do, and He re - wards those who seek Him.

15

God Calls Us

(Matt. 9:36-38; John 20:21)

LINDA REBUCK

TOM FETTKE

*1. Be - cause so man - y need to know, It's
2. Be - cause so man - y need to see, That
*3. Be - cause so man - y need to hear, I

up to you and me to go. Be -
God a - lone can make them free; Be -
want to be a vol - un - teer. Be -

cause so man - y need to know, God
cause so man - y need to see, God
cause so man - y need to hear, God

calls us, God calls us.

16   Philippians 4:13

H. W. G.

HOMER W. GRIMES

17 I'm Gonna Hide God's Word Inside My Heart

(Ps. 119:11)

P. J. and H. J.

PETER and HANNEKE JACOBS

I'm gon - na hide God's Word in - side my

heart And learn each verse from mem - o -

18 God Gave Us a Special Book

R.P., J.H., and T.M.   (2 Tim.3:16)   RHETT PARRISH, JODI HANNA, and TRISH MENDOZA
Arr. by Ed Kee

A Lamp to My Feet

19

B.D.

(Ps. 119:105)

BEVERLY DARNALL

A lamp to my feet, a light to my path; It leads me wher-ev-er I go. A lamp to my feet, a light to my path: The won-der-ful Word of the Lord.

20 Sandy Land

(Matt. 7:24-27)

K. L.

KAREN LAFFERTY

Don't build your house on the sand-y land,_____ Don't build it too near the shore._____ Well, it might look kind of nice, but you'll have to build it twice; Oh, you'll have to build your house once more. more. You bet-ter build your house___ up-on a rock, Make a good foun-da-tion on a sol-id spot.___ Oh, the storms may come and go,_____ But the

peace of God you will know. more. Well, it might look kind of nice, but you'll

have to build it twice; Oh, you'll have to build your house once more.

21 Peter, James, and John in a Sailboat

(Luke 5:1-7)

Traditional

Arr. by Lyndell Leatherman

Traditional

1. Pe - ter, James, and   John in a sail - boat;   Pe - ter, James, and   John in a sail - boat;
2. Fished all night and   caught no___fish - es,   Fished all night and   caught no___fish - es,
3. Christ came walk - ing   down by the wa - ter,   Christ came walk - ing   down by the wa - ter,
4. Now their nets are   full and___break - ing,   Now their nets are   full and___break - ing,
5. Called their friends to   come and___help them,   Called their friends to   come and___help them,

Pe - ter, James, and   John in a sail - boat,   Down by the deep, deep   sea.
Fished all night and   caught no___fish - es,   Down by the deep, deep   sea.
Christ came walk - ing   down by the wa - ter,   Down by the deep, deep   sea.
Now their nets are   full and___break - ing,   Down by the deep, deep   sea.
Called their friends to   come and___help them,   Down by the deep, deep   sea.

Option: Arrange chairs in the shape of a boat.

Vs. 1: Sing only.
Vs. 2: Pretend to be fishing.
Vs. 3: Appoint "Christ" to walk around the "boat."
Vs. 4: Struggle with heavy nets.
Vs. 5: Cup hands to mouth as though calling.

22 Actions Speak Louder Than Words

K.H.

(James 1:22)

KATHIE HILL

23 Hallelujah!

Traditional

(Ps.150:6)

Traditional
Arr. by Joseph Linn

Hal-le - lu, hal-le-lu, hal-le - lu, hal-le-lu - jah! Praise ye the Lord! Hal - le - lu, hal-le - lu, hal -le - lu, hal-le-lu - jah! Praise ye the Lord. Praise ye the Lord, hal-le-lu - jah! Praise ye the Lord, hal-le-lu - jah! Praise ye the Lord, hal -le-lu - jah! Praise ye the Lord.

24 Love Is Patient

LYNNE BROWER and
CAROL McMILLEN

(1 Cor. 13:4-5)

Traditional Tune

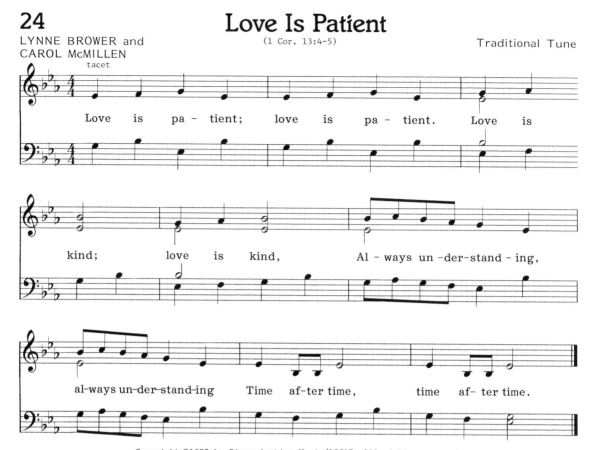

Love is pa-tient; love is pa-tient. Love is
kind; love is kind, Al-ways un-der-stand-ing,
al-ways un-der-stand-ing Time af-ter time, time af-ter time.

25 Gifts in My Heart

B.H.

(Ps. 116:12-14)

BETSY HERNANDEZ

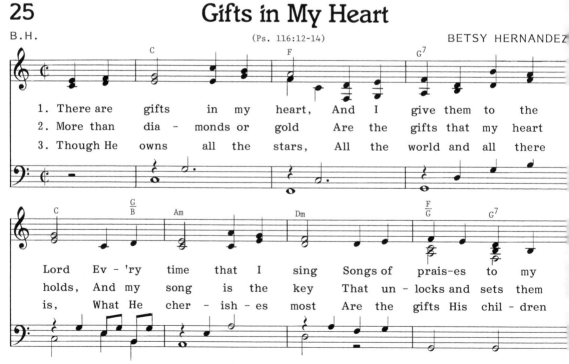

1. There are gifts in my heart, And I give them to the
2. More than dia-monds or gold Are the gifts that my heart
3. Though He owns all the stars, All the world and all there

Lord Ev-'ry time that I sing Songs of prais-es to my
holds, And my song is the key That un-locks and sets them
is, What He cher-ish-es most Are the gifts His chil-dren

26 Love the Lord

K.H.

(Deut.6:5)

KATHIE HILL

27 I Will Sing, I Will Sing

(Ps.146:1-2)

M.D.

MAX DYER

1. I will sing, I will sing a song___ un-to the Lord. I will
2. Al-le-lu, al-le-lu - ia, glo - ry to the Lord. Al-le-

sing, I will sing a song___ un-to the Lord. I will
lu, al-le-lu - ia, glo - ry to the Lord. Al-le-

sing, I will sing a song___ un-to the Lord; Al-le-
lu, al-le-lu - ia, glo - ry to the Lord; Al-le-

lu - ia, glo - ry to the Lord.
lu - ia, glo - ry to the Lord.

28   If You're Happy

Traditional   (Prov. 15:13)   Traditional
Arr. by Lyndell Leatherman

If you're hap-py and you know it, *clap your hands. *(clap, clap)* If you're hap-py and you know it, *clap your hands. *(clap, clap)* If you're hap-py and you know it, then your face will sure-ly show it. If you're hap-py and you know it, clap your hands. *(clap, clap)*

*Substitute: stamp your feet, say amen, do all three.

29   I Wonder How It Felt

(Gen. 6-8; Ex. 2:1-10; 1 Sam. 17; Prov. 3:5-6; Dan. 6; Jon. 1; Acts 16:23-24)

W. J. G. and GLORIA GAITHER   WILLIAM J. GAITHER

*1. I won-der how it felt to wake up in the bel-ly of a whale.
(2.) I won-der how it felt to meet___ big Go-li-ath in the field.
*(3.) I won-der how it'd be to watch your ba-by broth-er in the Nile;
*(4.) I won-der how it felt to spend the night with No-ah in the zoo;

I won-der how it felt to
I won-der how it felt to
I won-der who would come, a
I won-der how it felt to

*Verses 1, 3, 4 on recording.

spend the night with Si - las in the jail.
know the mouths of li - ons have been sealed.
prin - cess or a hun - gry croc - o - dile.
sleep be - side a smell - y kan - ga - roo.

I'm just a child, my life is still be - fore me; I just can't

wait to see what God has for me. But I know that I will trust Him, And I'll

wait to see what life will be for me.

2. I
3. I
4. I

me.

30 Everything That Is, Is His

(1 Chron. 29:14; Ps. 24:1-2)

KATHIE HILL

DAVID HAMPTON

Ev - 'ry-thing that is, is His; All that's un - der and be - side us, the Fa - ther has sup - plied us.

God's still the own - er; He's just loan - ing it, you see, 'Cause ev - 'ry-thing that is, is His!

last time to Coda

31
Seek Ye First
(Matt. 6:33)

K. L.

KAREN LAFFERTY

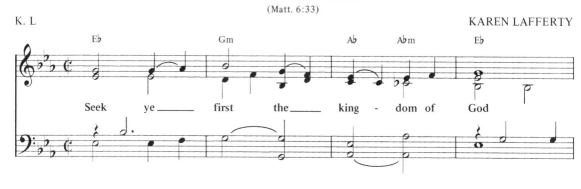

Seek ye ____ first the ____ king - dom of God

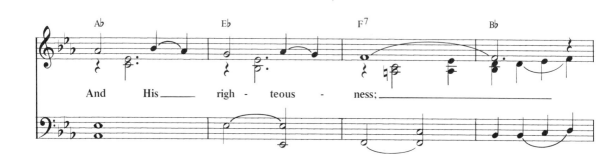

And His ____ righ - teous - ness; ____

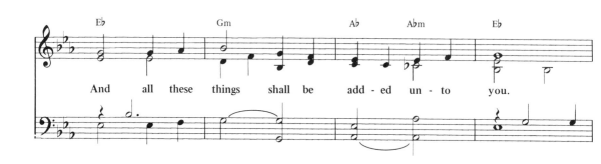

And all these things shall be add - ed un - to you.

Hal - le - lu, hal - le - lu - jah.

32 In My Father's House

(John 14:1-3)

Traditional

Traditional
Arr. by Joseph Linn

*1. Come and go with me to my Fa-ther's house, to my Fa-ther's house,
2. It's not ver-y far to my Father's house, to my Fa-ther's house,
*3. Je-sus is the way to my Father's house, to my Fa-ther's house,

to my Fa-ther's house. Come and go with me to my Fa-ther's
to my Fa-ther's house. It's not ver-y far to my Fa-ther's
to my Fa-ther's house. Je-sus is the way to my Fa-ther's

house where there's joy, joy, joy.
house where there's joy, joy, joy.
house where there's joy, joy, joy.

Optional final ending

joy, joy, joy, joy.

Optional verses:
4. Jesus is the Light in my Father's house . . .
5. All is peace and love in my Father's house . . .
6. We shall praise the Lord in my Father's house . . .

*Verses 1 & 3 on recording (with optional final ending).

33 He'll Be Comin' Down from Heaven

DOUG JOHNSON, age 9   (Matt. 24:30-31)

Traditional
Arr. by Steve Reynolds

1. He'll be com-in' down from heav-en when He comes; He'll be com-in' down from heav-en when He comes. He'll be com-in' down from heav-en, He'll be com-in' down from heav-en; He'll be com-in' down from heav-en when He comes.
2. He will come down in a cloud when He comes; He will come down in a cloud when He comes. He will come down in a cloud, He will come down in a cloud; He will come down in a cloud when He comes.
3. You will hear some trum-pets blow-ing when He comes; You will hear some trum-pets blow-ing when He comes. You will hear some trum-pets blow-ing, you will hear some trum-pets blow-ing; You will hear some trum-pets blow-ing when He comes.
4. All the an-gels will be sing-ing when He comes; All the an-gels will be sing-ing when He comes. All the an-gels will be sing-ing, all the an-gels will be sing-ing; All the an-gels will be sing-ing when He comes.

34 My Hands Belong to You

(Ps.63:4; 1 Cor.6:19-20)

A.W. and F.H.

ANE WEBER and FRANK HERNANDEZ

1. My hands be - long
2. My voice be - longs to You, Lord; My
3. My heart be - longs

hands be - long
voice be - longs to You._____ I
heart be - longs

them
lift it up to You, Lord, and sing
it

hal - le - lu - jah. I lift it up to
them
it

You, Lord, and sing hal - le - lu - jah._____

35

Adam, Adam

(Gen. 1-2, 6-9; Exod. 14; 1 Sam. 17; Jonah 1-2; Dan. 3,6)

R.P., J.H., and E.K.

RHETT PARRISH, JODI HANNA, and ED KEE
Arr. by Ed Kee

*1. A-dam, A-dam, won't you tell us
*2. No-ah, No-ah, won't you tell us
3. Mo-ses, Mo-ses, won't you tell us

how did you like par - a - dise? "God pro-vid - ed all I need-ed;
how'd you ev - er build that boat? "God pro-vid - ed all I need-ed;
how'd you ev - er part the seas? "God pro-vid - ed all I need-ed;

while it last-ed it was nice!"
thro' the storm I stayed a-float."
with His help it was a breeze."

*4. Da - vid, Da -vid, won't you tell us   how'd you kill that Phil - is - tine?
5. Shad-rach, Shad-rach, won't you tell us   how did you es - cape those flames?

"God pro-vid - ed all I need - ed   with five peb-bles and a sling."
"God pro-vid - ed all I need - ed;   all I did was call His name."

*Verses 1,2,4,6,8 on recording.

*6. Dan-iel, Dan-iel,
7. Jo-nah, Jo-nah,

won't you tell us   how'd you face that li-on's den? "God pro-vid-ed   all   I need-ed;
won't you tell us   how'd you live in-side that whale?"God pro-vid-ed   all   I need-ed;

soon those cats be-came my friends."
let   me live to tell the tale."

*8. Chris-tian, Chris-tian, let us tell you   how to fin-ish an - y task. God's pro-vid-ed

all you need, so   all you have to do is ask.

36 Teach Me, Lord

LINDA REBUCK

(1 Sam.3:10; Ps.25:4-5)

TOM FETTKE

37 He's Got the Whole World in His Hands

Spiritual

(Job 12:10; Ps.95:4)

Spiritual
Arr. by Lyndell Leatherman

With a shuffle

1. He's got the whole_____ world_____ in His hands;__ He's got the
2. He's got the wind and rain_____ in His hands;__ He's got the
3. He's got_____ you and me_____ in His hands;__ He's got_____
4. He's got_____ ev - 'ry - bod - y_____ in His hands;__ He's got_____

whole wide world_____ in His hands;_____ He's got the
wind and rain_____ in His hands;_____ He's got the
you and me_____ in His hands;_____ He's got_____
ev - 'ry - bod - y_____ in His hands;_____ He's got_____

whole_____ world_____ in His hands.__ He's got the
wind and rain_____ in His hands.__ He's got the
you and me_____ in His hands.__ He's got the
ev - 'ry - bod - y_____ in His hands.__ He's got the

whole world in His hands._____
whole world in His hands._____
whole world in His hands._____
whole world in His hands._____

38

Kids Under Construction
(Phil. 1:6)

GLORIA GAITHER and G. S. P.   WILLIAM J. GAITHER and GARY S. PAXTON

Kids un - der con - struc - tion;

May - be the paint is still wet.

Kids un - der con - struc - tion; The

39

Arky, Arky

Traditional

(Gen. 6-9)

Traditional

1. The Lord____ told No - ah, "There's gonna be___ a flood-y, flood-y."
(2. The) Lord____ told No - ah to build him___ an ark-y, ark-y.
3. The an-i-mals, the an-i-mals they came in___ by two-sies, two-sies.
(4. It) rained____ and poured____ for for - ty day-sies, day-sies.
5. The sun____ came out____ and dried up___ the land-y, land-y.

Lord____ told No-ah, "There's gon-na be___ a flood-y, flood-y." Get those an-i-mals
Lord____ told No-ah to build him___ an ark-y, ark-y. Build it out__ of
An-i-mals, the an-i-mals, they came in___ by two-sies, two-sies; El - e - phants and
Rained____ and poured____ for for - ty day-sies, day-sies; Al-most drove those
Sun____ came out____ and dried up___ the land-y, land-y. Ev - 'ry-thing__ was

out of the mud-dy, mud-dy,
go - pher bark-y, bark-y,
kan - ga-roo-sies, roo-sies, Chil-dren of the Lord.
an - imals cra-zy, cra-zy,
fine__ and dand-y, dand-y,

2. The
4. It

1,3

2,4,5

Lord. So rise____ and shine,____ and give God the glo-ry, glo-ry;

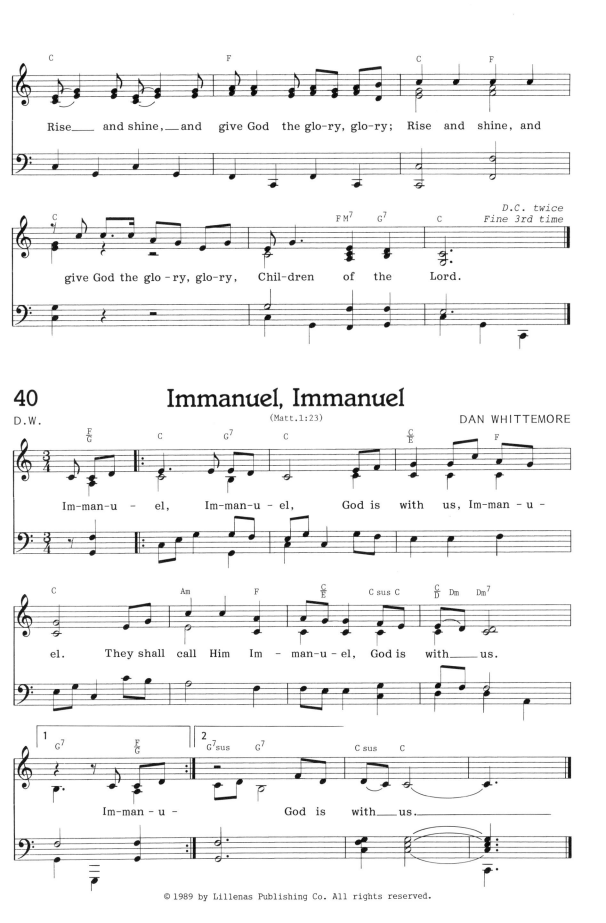

Rise___ and shine,___and give God the glo-ry, glo-ry; Rise and shine, and

give God the glo-ry, glo-ry, Chil-dren of the Lord.

D.C. twice
Fine 3rd time

40 Immanuel, Immanuel

D.W.

(Matt.1:23)

DAN WHITTEMORE

Im-man-u – el, Im-man-u – el, God is with us, Im-man – u –

el. They shall call Him Im – man-u – el, God is with___ us.

Im-man – u – God is with___us.___

41 Come On, Ring Those Bells

(Luke 2:1-14)

A.C.

ANDREW CULVERWELL

1. Ev-'ry-bod-y likes to take a hol-i-day; ev-'ry-bod-y likes to take a rest, Spend-ing time to-geth-er with the fam-i-ly, shar-ing lots of love and hap-pi-ness.

2. Cel-e-bra-tions come be-cause of some-thing good, cel-e-bra-tions we love to re-call. Mar-y had a ba-by boy in Beth-le-hem, the great-est cel-e-bra-tion of them all.

Come on, ring those bells; light the Christ-mas tree. Je-sus is the King born for you and me.

Come on, ring those bells; ev - 'ry-bod - y say,

"Je - sus, we re - mem - ber this Your birth - day."

42 Glory to God in the Highest

(Luke 2:14)

J.B. and R.E.L.   JOANNE BARRETT and RON E. LONG

Glo -ry to God in the high - est! Glo -ry to God

in the high - est heav - en. Glo - ry to God in the

high - est, And peace to men of good will.

43 Bethlehem Lullaby

(Luke 2:1-14)

P.W. BLACKNER

JOHANNES BRAHMS
Arr. by Lyndell Leatherman

1. Long a - go there was born in the cit - y of Da - vid a_____ sweet, ho - ly_____ Babe who was Je - sus, our King. An - gels sang at His birth, "Lul - la - by, peace on earth." An - gels sang at His birth, "Lul - la - by,_____ peace on earth."

2. Je - sus came as a child from His Fa - ther in heav - en and has shown us the_____ way to be lov - ing and kind, While the stars sang a - bove, "Lul - la - by, God is love"; While the stars sang a - bove, "Lul - la - by,_____ God is love."

When He Came

44

(Luke 2:10-14; 1 Peter 1:3; 1 John 4:9-10)

M.L.

MOSIE LISTER

1. He brought joy to the world when He came.
2. He brought peace to the world when He came.
3. He brought love to the world when He came.
4. He brought hope to the world when He came.

He brought joy to the world when He came.
He brought peace to the world when He came.
He brought love to the world when He came.
He brought hope to the world when He came.

To the hearts heav-y bur-dened with trou-bles and with
To the man-y and the few, and e-ven me and
Love that lives be-yond the grave, my soul and yours to
To the rich man, to the poor man, the beg-gar, and the

strife, He brought joy, great joy when He came.
you, He brought peace, last-ing peace when He came.
save, He brought love, won-drous love when He came.
king, He brought hope, liv-ing hope when He came.

45 His Name Is Life

(Ps.18:2; Isa.9:6; Matt.21:9; John 1:36-38; 4:42; 10:11; 14:6; 1 Cor.2:8; Rev.5:5; 15:3)

C.L.

CARMAN LICCIARDELLO and WILLIAM J. GAITHER

His name is Mas-ter, Sav-ior, Li - on of Ju - dah, Bless - ed Prince of__ Peace._____ Shep-herd, For - tress, Rock of sal - va - tion, Lamb of God is__ He. Son of Da - vid,

King of the A - ges, E - ter - nal Life; Ho - ly Lord of glo - ry, His name is Life.

46 O Come, Let Us Adore Him

(Ps.95:1,6; Rev.5:12)

Traditional

Wade's *Cantus Diversi*
Arr. by Lyndell Leatherman

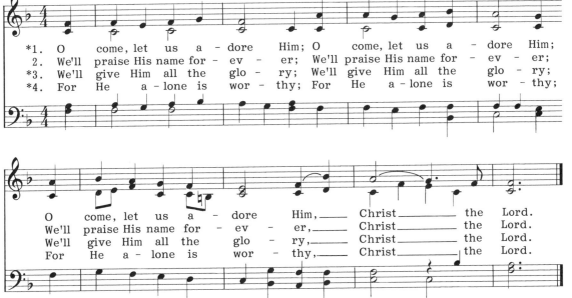

*1. O come, let us a - dore Him; O come, let us a - dore Him;
2. We'll praise His name for - ev - er; We'll praise His name for - ev - er;
*3. We'll give Him all the glo - ry; We'll give Him all the glo - ry;
*4. For He a - lone is wor - thy; For He a - lone is wor - thy;

O come, let us a - dore Him, Christ the Lord.
We'll praise His name for - ev - er, Christ the Lord.
We'll give Him all the glo - ry, Christ the Lord.
For He a - lone is wor - thy, Christ the Lord.

*Verses 1,3, and 4 on recording.

47

Amen!

Traditional

(Luke 2, 22-24; John 6:1-15)

Traditional Spiritual
Arr. by Lyndell Leatherman

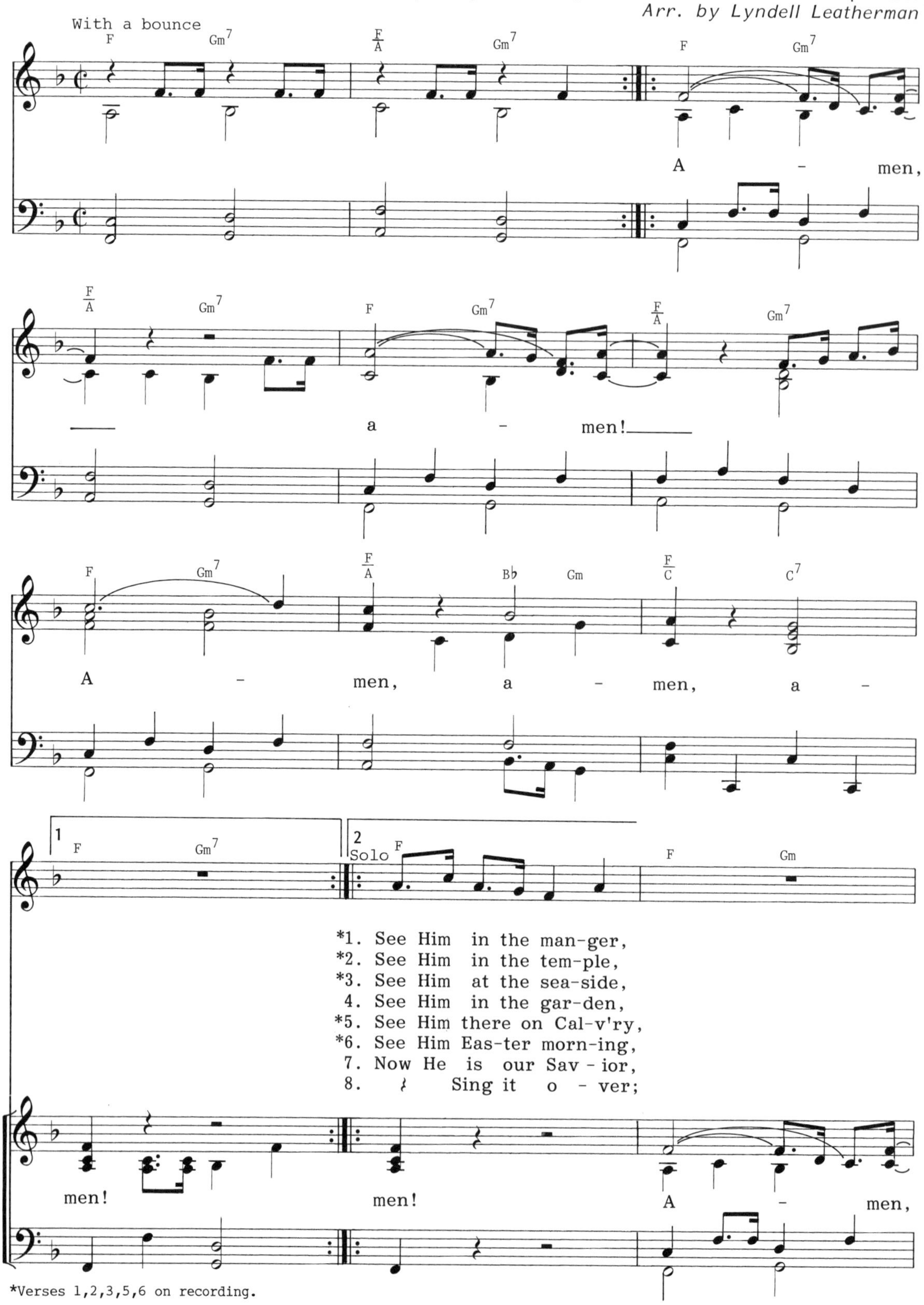

With a bounce
F Gm7 F/A Gm7 F Gm7
A - men,
F/A Gm7 F Gm7 F/A Gm7
a - men!
F Gm7 F/A B♭ Gm F/C C7
A - men, a - men, a -
1 F Gm7
2 Solo F
F Gm
*1. See Him in the man-ger,
*2. See Him in the tem-ple,
*3. See Him at the sea-side,
4. See Him in the gar-den,
*5. See Him there on Cal-v'ry,
*6. See Him Eas-ter morn-ing,
7. Now He is our Sav - ior,
8. Sing it o - ver;
men! men! A - men,

*Verses 1,2,3,5,6 on recording.

just   a lit-tle ba - by: Hear the an-gels sing - ing!
talk - in' to the el - ders: Mar - vel at His wis - dom!
preach-ing 'bout the king-dom: Mir - a-cles and won - ders!
bowed in deep-est sor - row: Pray-ing to His Fa - ther!
dy - ing for our sins:____   Lov-ing and for- giv - ing!
ris - en from the dead:____   He will live for-ev - er!
and His name is Je - sus: Glo-ry, hal-le- lu - jah!
      sing it o - ver: Glo-ry, hal-le- lu - jah!

a - men!____

(last time only)

A - men, a -

A - men, a - men, a -

great rit.

men, a - men!

men, a - men!

Enough Love

(John 3:16)

LINDA REBUCK

TOM FETTKE

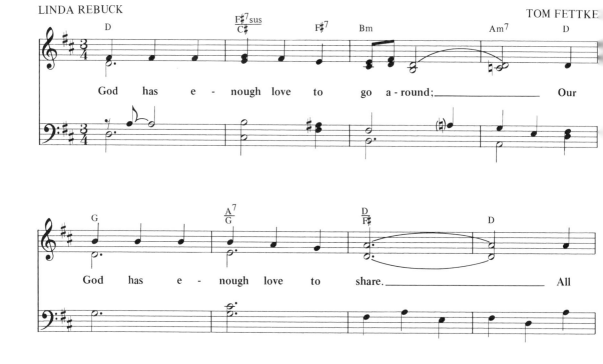

God has e - nough love to go a - round;_____ Our

God has e - nough love to share._____ All

o - ver the world His chil - dren are found Re-

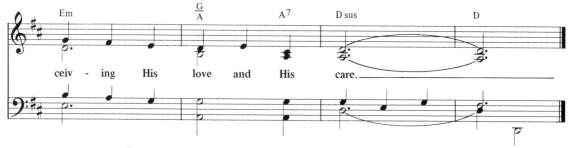

ceiv - ing His love and His care._____

49 Oh, How He Loves You and Me

K.K.

(John 15:13; 1 John 4:9-10)

KURT KAISER

50 Children, Join the Celebration

(Matt. 28:5-7)

J.E.P.

JOE E. PARKS

1. Chil - dren join ___ the cel - e - bra - tion on this hap - py Eas - ter day; Christ the Lord is ris - en as He said!
2. Praise Him now ___ with songs of glad - ness; sing tri - um - phant hymns of praise; Christ the Lord is ris - en as He said!

Ma - ry, on ___ that ear - ly morn - ing, heard the an - gel glad - ly say:
Chil - dren, join ___ the cel - e - bra - tion, with the hosts ___ of heav - en say:

"Je - sus lives— He is no long - er dead!"
"Je - sus Christ, our

Sav - ior, lives to - day."

51

Be Strong

KENT ASHLEY

(Josh. 1:9)

Traditional
Arr. by Lyndell Leatherman

1. Be strong and cou - ra - geous and bold,_____ Be
2. He's with you wher - ev - er you go,_____ He's
3. So trust Him with all of your heart,_____ So

strong and cou - ra - geous and bold._____ A - way with your fear, for
with you wher - ev - er you go._____ He's there by your side to
trust Him with all of your heart._____ Be - lieve and o - bey each

God will be near. Be strong and cou - ra - geous and bold._____
help and to guide. He's with you wher-ev-er you go._____
hour of the day, And trust Him with all of your heart._____

52

You Are Lord to Me

T. McL.

(Isa.9:6; Mark 4:39; 1 Cor.2:8; Col.1:27; Rev.22:16)

TOM McLAIN

You are my Lord; You give life to me.

You give me hope; You're my Prince of Peace.

You cause the winds and the waves to cease;

You are___ Lord to me.

You are the Lord of glo - ry;___

You are the Prince_____ of Peace.

You are the Bright and Morn – ing Star;

You_____ are Lord to me._____

"He will be called Wonderful Counselor, Mighty God, Everlasting Father, Prince of Peace" (Isaiah 9:6, NIV).

"Christ in you, the hope of glory" (Colossians 1:27, NIV).

"I am the Root and the Offspring of David, and the bright Morning Star" (Revelation 22:16, NIV).

53 We Are the Light

T.McL.

(Matt.5:13-16)

TOM McLAIN

54 Give It to Jesus

use me as He will, then I glad - ly will give Him my all.

55 What a Mighty God We Serve

(Isa. 60:16)

Unknown

Unknown
Arr. by Lyndell Leatherman

What a might - y God we serve.____

What a might - y God we serve.____

An - gels bow be - fore____ Him;____ Heav'n and earth a - dore____ Him.____

____ What a might - y God we serve.____

56

O. S.

Jesus, I Love You

(Ps. 116:1; 2 Cor. 5:14-15)

OTIS SKILLINGS

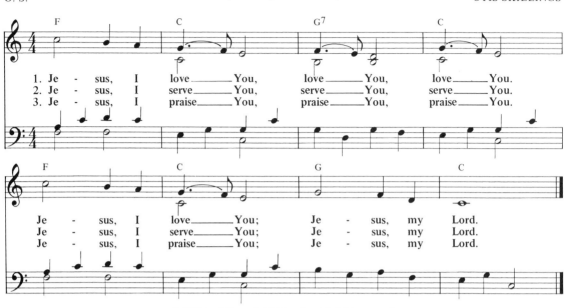

1. Je - sus, I love _____ You, love _____ You, love _____ You.
2. Je - sus, I serve _____ You, serve _____ You, serve _____ You.
3. Je - sus, I praise _____ You, praise _____ You, praise _____ You.

Je - sus, I love _____ You; Je - sus, my Lord.
Je - sus, I serve _____ You; Je - sus, my Lord.
Je - sus, I praise _____ You; Je - sus, my Lord.

57

C. K.

No Mountain High Enough

(Rom. 8:35-39)

CHARLES KIRBY

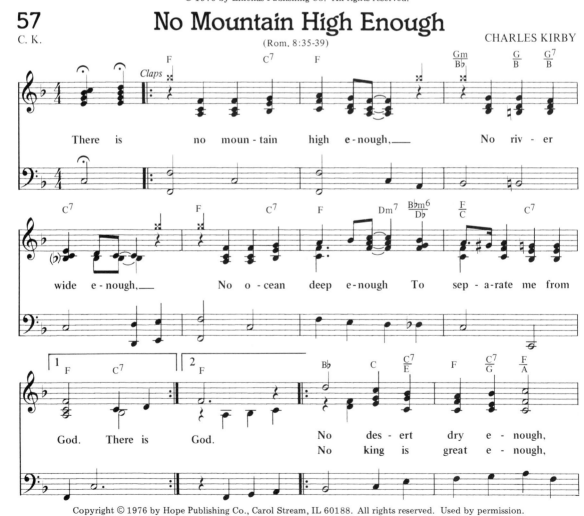

There is no moun - tain high e - nough, _____ No riv - er

wide e - nough, _____ No o - cean deep e - nough To sep - a - rate me from

God. There is God.

No des - ert dry e - nough,
No king is great e - nough,

58 We Are the Children

(1 Cor. 15:3-4; 1 Peter 1:18-19; 1 John 3:1)

T. McL.

TOM McLAIN

We are the chil-dren of___ the King.___ We want to laugh and we want ___ to sing.___ We want to share___ the joy - ful news___ That Je - sus Christ___ is call - ing you.

3rd time: fine

1. All   o - ver the world,___   the
2. We   are___ His own;___   He has

mes - sage is   the same:___   He died___ for you,
bought us with   a price—___   His pre-cious blood,

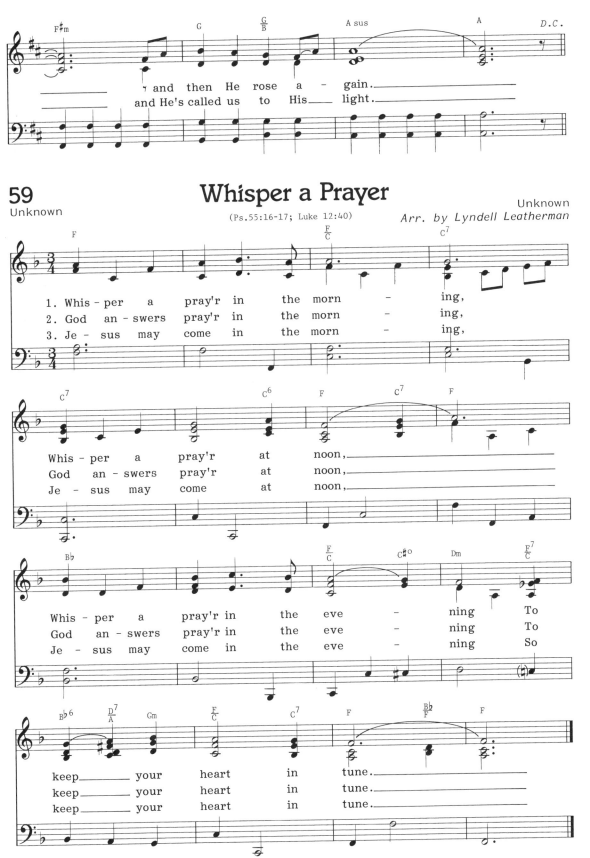

Whisper a Prayer

59
Unknown

(Ps.55:16-17; Luke 12:40)

Unknown
Arr. by Lyndell Leatherman

1. Whis-per a pray'r in the morn - ing,
2. God an-swers pray'r in the morn - ing,
3. Je-sus may come in the morn - ing,

Whis-per a pray'r at noon,
God an-swers pray'r at noon,
Je-sus may come at noon,

Whis-per a pray'r in the eve - ning To
God an-swers pray'r in the eve - ning To
Je-sus may come in the eve - ning So

keep your heart in tune.
keep your heart in tune.
keep your heart in tune.

and then He rose a - gain.
and He's called us to His light.

60 When We Talk to Him

(Ps. 34:15, 17; 145:18)

D. S.

DAVID STEELE

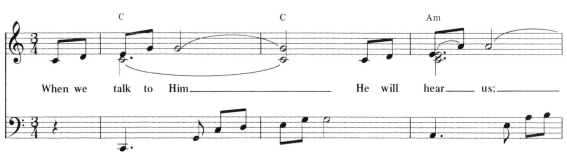

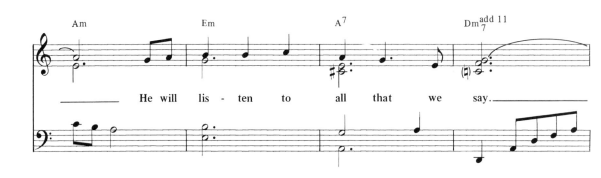

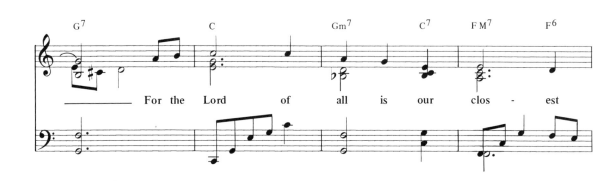

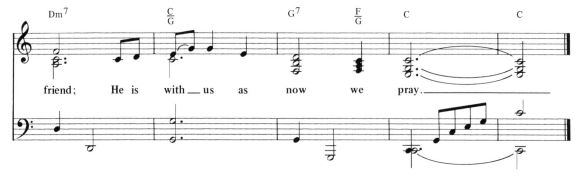

TOPICAL INDEX

ALPHABETICAL INDEX